Fundraising Realities
Every Board Member Must Face

A 1-Hour Crash Course on Raising Major Gifts
for Nonprofit Organizations

SECOND EDITION

First printed February 2013

10 9 8 7 6 5 4 3

Printed in the United States of America
This text is printed on acid-free paper.

Copies of this book are available from the publisher
at discount when purchased in quantity for boards,
volunteers, or staff.

Emerson & Church, Publishers
15 Brook Street, Medfield, MA 02052
Tel. 508-359-0019 • Fax 508-359-2703
www.emersonandchurch.com

Library of Congress Cataloging-in-Publication Data

Lansdowne, David.
   Fundraising realities every board member must face : a 1-hour
crash course on raising major gifts for nonprofit organizations /
David Lansdowne. — Second Edition.
      pages cm
   Spine title: Fund raising realities
   ISBN 978-1-889102-03-0 (pbk. : alk. paper) 1. Fund raising—
United States. 2. Nonprofit organizations—United States—Finance.
I. Title. II. Title: Fund raising realities.
   HG177.5.U6L36 2013
   658.15'224—dc23
                                        2012032512

FOREWORD BY **JEROLD PANAS**

Fundraising Realities

EVERY BOARD MEMBER MUST FACE

SECOND EDITION

David Lansdowne

A **1-Hour** CRASH COURSE
On Raising Major Gifts for Nonprofit Organizations

Emerson
& Church
PUBLISHERS

The Bestselling Fundraising Book of All Time

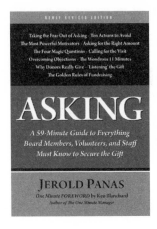

ASKING
by Jerold Panas

ASKING
A 59-Minute Guide to Everything
Board Members, Volunteers & Staff
Must Know to Secure the Gift

It ranks right up there with public speaking. Nearly all of us fear it.

And yet it's critical to our success.

Asking for money. It makes even the stout-hearted quivver.

But now comes a book, *Asking: A 59-Minute Guide to Everything Board Members, Volunteers, and Staff Must Know to Secure the Gift.* And short of a magic elixir, it's the next best thing for emboldening you, your board, and your volunteers to ask with skill, finesse, and powerful results.

Jerold Panas, who as a staff person, board member, and volunteer has secured gifts ranging from $50 to $100 million, understands the art of asking better than virtually anyone in the world.

He has harnessed all of his knowledge and experience and produced what is now the bestselling fundraising book in history.

What *Asking* convincingly shows is that it doesn't take stellar communication skills to be an effective asker. Nearly everyone, regardless of their persuasive ability, can succeed if they follow Jerold Panas's proven guidelines.

www.emersonandchurch.com

To Kathy and Laura

You can't have one without the other.

FOREWORD

Fundraising Realities Every Board Member Must Face is one of the top-selling fundraising books of all time.

And now in this fully revised Second Edition, David Lansdowne has achieved the near-impossible.

He has transformed a classic work that has guided tens of thousands of board members and made it better. Significantly better.

David delves even deeper now, introducing us to a wide array of people and organizations. His voice is as infectious as ever as he makes every fundraising tenet come alive.

In my Foreword to the First Edition, I wrote:

"As far as fundraising verities are concerned, this book is the Koran, the Talmud, and Deuteronomy all rolled into one." These words apply more than ever.

This isn't theory. Or hearsay. This is fundraising as it should be practiced. Have your board members read - better yet, devour - these pages as soon as possible.

They'll find that *Fundraising Realities* is a roadmap they'll want to follow. The signposts are all in place. The extraordinary journey begins.

Author and Executive Partner   **Jerold Panas**
Jerold Panas, Linzy & Partners

CONTENTS

THE REALITIES

1

In Close Company

Gather a hundred people together, 18 years and older.

How many would you guess serve on a nonprofit board? Twelve? Twenty?

The correct answer is seven.

That means you're in select company – an altruist, really.

After a long day, you're willing to grab a sandwich and dash off to hear yet another dry report from the treasurer.

It's enough to make you nod off.

But staying alert as a board member isn't your central challenge. There's caffeine for that.

A more pivotal task awaits you - and that's raising money to further your organization's mission.

You're heard the business adage, "Nothing happens without a sale." A similar dynamic is at work here. Very little happens if you and your fellow board members don't marshal the resources your organization needs to thrive.

My hope is that *Fundraising Realities* makes that critical responsibility a little easier.

This book is intentionally brief, free of jargon, and takes a light hand as it spells out the do's and don'ts of raising more than pocket money.

It follows the process from beginning to end, from defining your mission to evaluating your results.

The ideas discussed here have been perfected over the past half-century by organizations large and small. From urban hospitals to local historical societies. To raise $100,000 and unthinkable sums like $100,000,000.

Needless to say, you can't raise amounts like that casually. There are prescribed steps to follow - proven methods to adopt. Still, there's something more essential than technique, and that's your doggedness to get the job done, whatever it takes.

Blend together the approach discussed in these pages with a heaping dose of your own personal grit, and there's your Julia Child recipe for success. Delicious and practically foolproof.

Some years ago Nicholas Meyer wrote a novel chronicling the adventures of Sherlock Holmes. Its title could well apply to you. In your (sometimes lonely) dedication to the cause, you yourself are part of *The Seven-Per-Cent Solution*.

NOTE: I've calculated the imperfect number seven using statistics drawn from the National Center for Charitable Statistics, the U.S. Census Bureau, BoardSource, and the Annie E. Casey Foundation.

2

The Mission Must Be Defined

"We will put a man on the moon by the end of the decade."

"Make Phoenix the safest major city."

"Establish ourselves as the premier purveyor of the finest coffee in the world."

There's no mistaking the mission behind these words of John Kennedy, the Phoenix Police Department, and Starbucks.

They don't say "We'll get near the moon," or "Make Phoenix cordial," or "Brew a good cup of Joe." Instead, they define a clear and specific goal.

As a board member, that's your charge, too, before embarking on a fundraising drive. You want distilled clarity on your organization's mission - and agreement by all.

It may take a half-day retreat or several board meetings to achieve this, as there are tough questions to answer:

- ❏ Why does our organization exist?
- ❏ What makes our organization better, or more effective, than similar ones?
- ❏ Are our priorities clear?
- ❏ What are our major strengths and weaknesses?
- ❏ How can we improve our services?
- ❏ What are our long- and short-range objectives? And,
- ❏ Where do our resources come from and are they sufficient?

And just because you've been around since Lincoln Logs doesn't mean you can ignore this step. The American Heart Association, founded in 1924, still reviews its mission regularly. In her book, *You've Gotta Have Heart*, Cass Wheeler, former CEO of the organization, tells why: "The environment changes and the organization changes, so a periodic review is important to ensure that there is alignment of purpose and reality."

You can be sure that would-be donors, before pledging sizable sums, will pose some tough questions. If you hope to secure their support, you have to be able to articulate your mission and describe viable plans for reaching your goals.

3

The Buck Starts Here

Every field has its first principles. You might call them axioms to live by.

For Apple Computer, Steve Jobs's mantra was "No Compromises."

For serious journalists, the first obligation is to the truth.

Physicians since the 5th century BC have been guided by the words of Hippocrates: "First do no harm."

Fundraising, too, has a first principle. It is that boards have an obligation to give and to get.

The "get" part we'll cover in later chapters. Here, let's focus on board giving.

Some organizations actually prescribe a giving level for board members. One prominent college recommends a gift equal to its yearly tuition. An established arts center suggests $50,000 per year. More affordable is the request from a mid-Atlantic advocacy group: $2,500.

That's one bold approach. The more common one is for organizations simply to encourage each board member to make a *generous* gift. Some go so far as to spell out what generous means in the job description: "While serving on the board, I commit to making our organization one of the top three charities I support each year."

Regardless of your organization's approach, your gift is critical.

First, by virtue of your position, you are expected - by the staff and by the community at large – to be the organization's steadfast supporter. Can you legitimately expect others to give generously if you won't?

Second, your gift is tangible evidence of your commitment. Nothing says "I believe in this cause" more convincingly than writing a check.

Third, your generous gift gives you standing as a solicitor. "This cause is so important, Tom, that my wife and I have pledged $5,000. I'm hoping you and Alicia will join us in making a gift." Your credibility is undermined if you have to say to your prospective donor, "To tell you the truth, I haven't given anything myself."

It may not be what you expected when you came aboard. And probably you can list a dozen reasons why giving right at this moment is inconvenient. But you accepted the job and what comes with it.

Make your gift, if you haven't already. You'll feel good; and you'll smell good, too. You have it on the word of Confucius: "A bit of fragrance always clings to the hand that gives roses."

4

Most Everyone Dislikes Asking

According to the Anxiety Disorders Association of America, 19 million people have specific phobias.

The most common include fears of snakes, spiders, heights, and water. Fear of public speaking and fear of flying are also widespread.

But I'm sure the ADAA slipped up. The fear of asking for money isn't even in the top 30, which is crazy, since every executive director and development officer in the land will confirm that countless volunteers suffer from it.

In fact, we'll summon just about any excuse to avoid asking:
- I give my time, that's enough.
- I don't know the right people.
- Fundraising is belittling.
- Raising money is the job of the development staff.
- If I ask, I know they'll ask me back.
- My Corolla needs washing.

But recall that board obligation to give and to get. Well,

raising money is the getting part. It's your organization. Its steward is that person you see in the mirror.

That means, among other things, asking friends, neighbors, and colleagues to join you in furthering the cause. If that fuels anxiety, you can either reach for Xanax or tamp your anxiety by keeping the following in mind:

❏ You aren't asking for yourself. That would be infinitely harder.
❏ You have nothing to gain financially.
❏ You've already testified to your own commitment by making a gift.

And, always remember that asking is like proposing to your girlfriend: you gotta be there. "We convince by our presence," is how Walt Whitman put it. Almost no one will give a large gift unless you stand before them and ask.

It makes sense, too. When's the last time YOU gave $25,000, or even $2,500 because the irresistible urge struck?

5

Be Ready or Regroup

Would you enter a marathon if running a mile left you gasping?

Would you hire yourself out as an electrician before knowing AC from DC?

Would you sit for a major job interview without first preparing?

Of course not. "Before everything else, getting ready is the secret of success," said Henry Ford.

Then, would you launch a fundraising campaign without considering the likelihood of success?

Of course you wouldn't. But all too often others in your position blindly press on. Which is curious since evaluating whether you're ready isn't that hard. All you have to do is satisfactorily answer a handful of questions:

- ❏ Are our organization's goals unmistakably clear?
- ❏ Are we seen as a worthy asset to our community, our city, our country?
- ❏ Do we believe the cause is important?
- ❏ Will we contribute time *and* money?

❏ Can we make a persuasive (and urgent) case for
   funding our project?
❏ Do we have leadership for the campaign,
   including a candidate for general chairperson?

And then the most pertinent question of all:

❏ Do we have enough legitimate prospects? That
   means three to four prospective donors for every
   one gift we hope to secure.

About this last question, don't kid yourself. Facebook's
Mark Zuckerberg may live across town, even next door, but
that's nothing more than a geographic oddity unless he's
already involved with your group.

You can charge ahead anyway. It's *possible* to attempt Mt.
Fuji in flip-flops. But reaching the summit is a different matter.
Until the entire board commits, and until you've identified
capable leadership and scores of prospects, you're well advised
to retreat and re-examine.

6

Money Costs Money

On average, U.S. couples spend nearly $26,000 for their nuptials, according to The Wedding Report (theweddingreport.com).

It doesn't have to be this way, of course. The Valley of Fire wedding package in Las Vegas, which includes a stretch limo, 100 photographs, an eight-inch round wedding cake *and* bottled water, can be yours for $999 (plus applicable taxes).

Much like weddings, fundraising costs run the gamut.

To begin with, you'll need money for operating costs, things like printing, postage, office space, additional staffing, transportation, and clerical help. Then there are pesky consulting fees (more on consultants later). These can range anywhere from a few hundred per month to $250,000 annually for full-service, on-site campaign management.

How much, specifically, should your campaign cost? It all depends, of course. Some established organizations spend less than 10 cents for every dollar they raise, while many new groups spend 50 cents or more.

So much is dictated by the following variables:

❏ The amount you're trying to raise.

❏ The number of prospects you've identified.

❏ Your plans for cultivating these individuals.

❏ Where your prospects live.

❏ Whether you'll be hiring an independent consultant or a full-service firm.

❏ The duration of your campaign. And,

❏ Your current level of support.

William Krueger, writing for capitalcampaigns.com, offers the following figures as a rule of thumb for large campaigns (these assume a consulting firm providing soup to nuts service – your costs for a smaller drive using an independent consultant could be less):

For a $2,000,000 campaign, expect to pay 8 to 15 percent of the goal.

For a $2,000,000 to $5,000,000 campaign, 7 to 12 percent.

For a $5,000,000 to $25,000,000 campaign, 4 to 8 percent.

Campaigns over $25,000,000 might be as little as 1 to 2 percent.

I might add that "little" in the preceding sentence is Krueger's word for $250,000 to $500,000, not mine.

7

Make Your Case

If I asked you, What is your purpose in life? that would be tough to answer. It's a question that's dogged everyone from Sophocles to Shakespeare to Oprah Winfrey.

However, if a potential donor asks you, What is your *organization's* purpose? you need an answer – a ready one.

❏ Why are you seeking funds?
❏ Why now?
❏ Why should I give to your organization and not another?
❏ Who will benefit?
❏ How will you know?

The answers to these questions should roll off your tongue.

And they will if before setting out to raise money you think through the rationale for your campaign and lay out your conclusions in a "case statement." In essence, this is your organization's reason for being.

It tells donors and prospects who you are, what you're trying to accomplish, and why. It describes your history, and purpose, and plans. But, most importantly, it offers compelling reasons to invest in your particular cause, *right now*, and who will benefit.

Your case statement needn't be long or elaborate. More important is that it's tasteful, well-written, free of hyperbole, and, here's the clincher, *written from the perspective of your potential donors.*

On this last key point listen to what case expert Tom Ahern, author of *Seeing Through a Donor's Eyes,* has to say: "Prospects want to be moved. I mean hearts-beating-faster moved, hairs-standing-on-end moved. You're not fundraisers as much as 'hope-raisers.' You're selling to donors the credible hope that they can change the world for the better … through you … if they invest in your merry band of troublemakers, change agents, teachers, healers, saints, or such."

If yours is a simple appeal for funds – "Local Prodigy Needs College Aid" - a single sheet could do. On the other hand, you might want a 12-page (frugally printed) brochure or PDF if your goal is to fund a new, $10 million wing to the city art museum.

What matters more than length or looks is your ability to convincingly answer the most pressing question on your would-be donor's mind: *Why should I give you my money now?*

8

Individuals Are The Target

Here's the math.

In the U.S., there are just over 120,000 private foundations, according to the National Center for Charitable Statistics. These include everything from the Carnegie Endowment to DoSomething.org.

In addition, there are 2,700 corporate foundations with household names like Bank of America and Coca Cola.

Sizable numbers, to be sure, but they pale in comparison to the estimated *140 million* adults who each and every year send checks to their alma mater or local museum or community hospital.

So it shouldn't surprise you that of the billions contributed annually to charity, roughly *85 percent* comes from individuals like you (90 percent if you include bequests, which come from individuals, too).

A big grant from Walmart or the Gates Foundation makes the headlines, but it's those millions of under-the-radar gifts that account for the bulk of philanthropy.

As a result, it makes sense to focus most of your attention on individuals.

Unfortunately, too many people ignore hard data and spend a disproportionate amount of time chasing corporations and foundations. Why? For two reasons, I suspect. First, these sources are the most obvious – you'll find them conveniently listed in various directories. Second, corporations and foundations *expect* to be solicited (many via the Web these days). That means the nail-biting element of fundraising – standing in front of someone and asking for a gift – is eliminated.

Granted, some organizations – about one in five according to a study reported in the *Stanford Social Innovation Review* - rely on corporate funding for a sizable share of their income. But keep your priorities straight by remembering three simple truths:

• Most private support comes from individuals. (A study by Bank of America and the Center for Philanthropy at Indiana University showed that 98.2 percent of high net worth households give to charity.)

• Much of our nation's wealth is in the form of real property, owned by individuals. And,

• Individuals don't have defined priorities; they can give to whatever they wish, whenever they wish.

9

A Few Contribute The Most

Pea pods tell you a lot about fundraising.

If you're a gardener, you know from experience that 80 percent of your peas come from 20 percent of your pods. The first person to observe this, at least on record, was Vilfredo Pareto (born 1848), a gardener in addition to engineer, sociologist, economist, and philosopher.

Today, the "Pareto Principle" is an accepted rule of thumb in business. It states – and your retail friends will confirm this - that 80 percent of a company's sales come from 20 percent of its customers.

Only in fundraising, the ratio's more skewed.

As borne out by decades of experience and literally thousands of campaigns, *90 percent* of the funds raised in a typical campaign come from just *10 percent* of the donors. A recent study by CASE (higher education's professional association) reaffirmed this ratio as the "canonical rule."

What it means is that to reach your goal you'll need to

devote most of your time – as much as 90 percent – to your top prospects, relying on sizable gifts from them.

Only don't ignore everyone else or you may come to regret it!

Consider that Mary Jean and Frank Smeal's first gift to Penn State's College of Liberal Arts was $5.00. More than 30 years later their *$10 million* gift ranked as the largest in the school's history.

Or take William and Joan Schreyer. Their $30 million gift built the Schreyer Honors College, also at Penn State. Their first check to the university 37 years earlier? That would be $10.

Lastly, listen to what Teresa Eyring, former director of the Children's Theatre of Minneapolis, told Minnesota Public Radio: "One day in the mail we received a check for $12 from a young person who attended the theater on a regular basis." Attached was a note saying this was "part of her savings and she thought it was very important for the children's theater to have this campaign."

You just know that 30 years from now you'll pick up the paper and read about a $5 million gift from a woman who scrimped as a child so she could donate $12 to a nearby theatre she thoroughly loved.

10

Think in Thirds

Blind mice. Wise men. Rock paper scissors. Many things come in groups of three.

That's true of donors, too. You will find, as countless others have, that your campaign's donors will fall into three separate categories.

Group one will contain your top 10 to 15 donors. From this small corps, you'll receive a third of your goal.

Group two will be your next 100 to 125 donors, from whom another third of your funds will come.

Group three will be everyone else - hundreds if not thousands of donors. The final third of your money will come from these individuals.

In fundraising, this is known as the Rule of Thirds, first codified by Harold J. ("Si") Seymour who authored the classic text, *Designs for Fund-Raising.*

For a $1 million campaign, the rule of thirds plotted on a "Gift Table" might look like the illustration on the next page:

Gift Amount	# of Gifts	Total Amount
$100,000	1	$100,000
$50,000	2	$100,000
$25,000	4	$100,000
$10,000	20	$200,000
$2,000	150	$300,000
Under $1,000	many	$200,000

Understand, the percentages will fluctuate. In fact, in recent years the trend is for the top 10 to 15 gifts to provide as much as *half* of the goal (the University of Texas at Austin raised 86 percent of its money from just *two* percent of the donors).

But unless you're surrounded by gushers (of the oil and donor types), you can with confidence develop your table of gifts with the Rule of Thirds in mind.

11

Interviews
Are Revealing

Play the slot machines at Las Vegas or Atlantic City and your odds of winning are as long as 1 in 33,000 (worse if it's a mega jackpot).

"What's with these paltry payouts!" you want to scream, as the cylinder slows to reveal yet another cherry … apple … banana. But no matter how much you bump and jostle, the slots are mum.

Thankfully, this isn't the case with *your* projected source of funding. You can actually speak with prospective donors. It's called a *feasibility study* or *planning study*.

The process is simple. First you hire a consultant (to ensure the objectivity of your study). Next you work with her to identify a range of people (board members, major gift prospects, business leaders, and community "pillars") who can make or influence large gifts. Lastly, the consultant goes out and interviews as many of these people as will see her.

While it won't guarantee the amount you can raise, a

carefully conducted feasibility study will:

- ❏ Uncover your organization's strengths and weaknesses.
- ❏ Help you set a campaign goal.
- ❏ Identify leaders and prospects for your campaign, including the level of gifts you might expect.
- ❏ Reveal what your community thinks of your organization or project.

Sometimes a study will suggest you suspend activities until corrective measures are taken.

For example, Drake University's feasibility study revealed the following: the school didn't have adequate prospects for a $200 million campaign; the fundraising message was blurry; the president wasn't focused enough on fundraising; and the vice president of alumni and development lacked experience.

Still, the university chose trial by fire. "The only way we were going to fix the shortcomings in our operation was to put ourselves in a pressure-filled environment," said development officer John P. Smith in an interview with *Inside Higher Ed.* "We knew there'd be a steep learning curve, that there would be mistakes and issues, but that was the best solution to get us to a stronger position."

Smith's strategy seems to have paid off, as the university has already raised more than half of its goal.

Drake's experience goes to show that a feasibility study can serve you well, even in unexpected ways. Considering the cost - $15,000 to $80,000 – you would certainly hope so.

12

Consultants Will And Won't

They've been the butt of jokes, for sure. Dilbert's Scott Adams, speaking of consultants, said this: "They have credibility because they're not dumb enough to work at your company."

Former aerospace executive Norman Augustine says "All too many consultants, when asked what is 2 and 2? respond, 'What do you have in mind?'"

Despite the ribbing, consultants can serve an instrumental role. Certainly this is the case with a major gifts campaign. The undertaking is simply too big for staff, given their other responsibilities.

So just what is the role of the fundraising consultant? Let's first clarify what it is *not*.

❏ It is *not* to solicit money for you. That's the role of the board and, in some cases, the staff.
❏ It is *not* to haul in hundreds of new prospects. The best ones you already know.

❏ It's *not* to replace the work of staff or board members. It is to supplement their work and enhance their knowledge.

In sum, the role of a consultant is *not* to raise money *for* you, it is to help *you* raise it. In this regard, what the seasoned consultant *will* do is:

❏ Help you evaluate your needs.
❏ Uncover your strengths and weaknesses.
❏ Assess your fundraising potential.
❏ Outline a plan of action (if you're ready).
❏ Help prepare materials.
❏ Conduct trainings.
❏ Troubleshoot. And,
❏ Serve as a catalyst to keep your campaign moving.

Can you succeed without a consultant? Absolutely. Some people purchase kits and build their own homes. Says *Mother Earth News*: "If you have lots of time, and are self-reliant, patient and a fast learner, you may be able to do much (or all) of the work yourself."

Simply read the directions and start pouring the foundation.

13

No Goal, No Objective

"**H**eck, let's just raise all we can. We don't need a goal."

If you're new to fundraising, you might consider this a sensible approach.

What can it hurt, right?

Nothing but your credibility.

"How much are you trying to raise?"

"Not sure."

"How much do you need?"

"Loads."

People won't take you seriously without a dollar goal. They'll also question your competence.

So how do you go about establishing a goal? It's a bit tricky. By that I mean you have to strike a delicate balance between A) what's feasible and, B) what's challenging.

On the one hand, potential donors have to view your goal as attainable (or they'll simply toss a few dollars your way). On the other hand, they must be inspired to make a stretch gift (USC's $6 *billion* campaign no doubt stretched donors all the way to Pluto).

Goal-setting demands you juggle a number of variables: your need for funds; the persuasiveness of your case; the financial capacity of your prospect list; your constituency's appreciation of your achievements; and the strength of your leadership.

Some will argue for a high goal, relishing the challenge.

Others will insist on a low, achievable goal that leaves everyone proud.

Still others will lobby for a goal reflecting the exact costs of the project.

Each side has merits. Which is right for you depends on the unique makeup of your group – its talents, ambitions, dreams, and dedication.

If you're nervous about announcing a goal – afraid you'll fail and be embarrassed - keep the counsel of Edmund Hillary, first to scale Everest, in mind: "It is not the mountain we conquer but ourselves."

14

Calling All Recruits

He's in the pantheon of history's most dedicated volunteers.

Michael Leto, former VP of alumni relations and development at Central Michigan University, will vouch for that.

CMU was in the middle of its $50 million capital campaign. A key meeting was scheduled, but a national emergency had grounded all flights. What's a distant alumnus to do?

Take to the road, of course. "This committee member," recalls Leto in a CMU campaign newsletter, "rented a car and drove 1,500 miles the day after the 9/11 terrorist attacks to attend our campaign meeting."

With that level of dedication, is it any wonder CMU shattered its original goal and raised $78 million?

Admittedly, that's setting the bar high, but stalwart volunteers are what your campaign needs. Scores of them.

Some will serve on subcommittees, others may help plan your kickoff or victory celebrations, still others may serve in a speakers' bureau to publicize your cause.

But the *pivotal* role volunteers play is increasing your capacity to ask for gifts. *In person.*

Heed those last two words.

Jerold Panas, who has consulted with nearly 3,000 boards and helped organizations raise literally billions of dollars, clarifies:

"You won't get a gift, at least not of the size you want, by sending a letter, calling on the phone, or worse, sending an email. You're going to have to visit your prospect in person."

To give you a sense of the person-power you'll need, a recent California Assistance League drive for $3.6 million involved more than *120 volunteers.*

A land trust agency in upstate New York raised its $1.3 million goal with the help of 140 volunteers.

A Baltimore health care agency serving the homeless required 160 volunteers to raise $2.6 million.

Just how much manpower you'll need depends on the appeal of your cause, the size of lead gifts, how well you've screened your would-be donors, and the skill of your solicitors.

One thing is certain, however; Hillary Clinton is right. It takes a village.

15

Those Who Set the Goal, Set Their Sights

"Do it because I say so!"

Whether as children or adults, we don't take kindly to those words. We want to know the reasoning. We also want a say.

Keep this dynamic in mind when deciding your dollar goal.

To a large extent it's your CEO's job to identify the resources you need. But once this background work is done, there's no better way to begin motivating your top campaign workers than to involve them in setting the goal.

When they have a say in the process, when they can voice their opinions and participate in the debate, they'll "own" the campaign and be markedly more committed.

Not that volunteers can do it alone. As we said earlier, setting a goal is challenging. Factors such as your organization's history, your prospect pool, the urgency of your project, the findings of your feasibility study, current income sources – all

43

of these will shape the final figure. Without staff or professional guidance, board members will often set goals that are too low or unattainably high.

But to exclude these key players is to lose a golden opportunity to cultivate the team spirit your campaign ultimately depends on. As Henry Ford said, "If everyone is moving forward together, then success takes care of itself."

16

Publicity Is No Substitute

"All publicity is good, except an obituary notice," said Irish poet Brendan Behan.

And while there's a measure of truth to the value of publicity, don't expect it to raise money. Except in extraordinary cases (think Katrina, the Indonesian Tsunami, the Japanese earthquake), it won't.

The reasons are probably clear to you by now. To raise substantial money, as we noted in Chapter 3, you have to call upon your prospects, regardless of any well-placed stories. Second, most campaigns depend on a relatively small number of major donors whose decision to give won't be influenced by the media. In fact, these prospects are approached during the "quiet phase" of a campaign, before anything has even been announced.

Consider that the University of Rochester was 63 percent of the way toward its goal before publicizing its campaign; Case Western Reserve had secured 66 percent.

Those who think publicity raises money tend to be novices or loosely committed volunteers. They hope the media will do the heavy lifting. When this doesn't happen, they blame the failure not on themselves but on the lack of exposure.

Consider a publicity drive only if one of the following applies:

- ❑ If you're using an event to raise money and need to sell a large number of tickets.
- ❑ If your project benefits the general public, such as the refurbishing of a community park.
- ❑ If you're persuaded that publicity will stimulate your leadership to work harder.
- ❑ If you have a number of big donors who would like the attention.
- ❑ If you have a weak image.
- ❑ If you've already raised most of your goal and want to stimulate your campaign workers to complete their calls.

But even when one or more of these factors exists, remember that publicity is always an adjunct measure. As a study by the University of Pennsylvania's Center for High Impact Philanthropy confirmed in interviews with major donors, "few made a practice of giving large gifts in situations where they had simply heard of and/or read about an organization." It was involvement in the cause that prompted their gift.

17

Special Events Can Be Double-Edged

Daniel Goleman, a psychologist who's written on the subject of emotional intelligence, says this: "The emotional brain responds to an event more quickly than the thinking brain."

If Goleman had said the emotional brain responds to a *special* event more quickly than the thinking brain, he would have been correct, too.

Like honeybees to nectar, volunteers are drawn to special events. Bring up the need to raise funds and almost on cue they'll suggest a dinner dance or road race or gala.

It seems like fun, and it's easy to get excited ... especially if you ignore the associated costs. Even when a good number of products and services are donated, you still need to cover the banquet hall, or greens fees, or police detail – and don't forget the catering. Factor in printing, flowers, decorations, music, perhaps even travel and lodging, and the costs rise quicker than champagne bubbles.

Think of it this way: a gala to benefit the local museum might raise $10,000 and consume literally 300 volunteer hours. You could devote a fraction of that time to identifying, cultivating, and soliciting a handful of high-potential donors and raise the same amount of money, if not more.

In terms of the relative effectiveness of fundraising methods, the late Henry Rosso, founder of The Fund Raising School, ranked special events near the very bottom, behind team soliciting, one-on-one soliciting, soliciting by personal letter with a follow-up phone call, and a personal telephone call by a peer with a follow-up letter.

Granted, there are valid reasons for holding an event: calling attention to your cause, educating and inspiring your current leaders and donors, attracting different factions of the community, and uncovering new constituents.

But before you schedule a Burp-a-Thon, make sure you plan well, have sufficient lead time, a realistic budget, ample numbers of volunteers, and the know-how to get your event widespread publicity.

Yes, and load up on carbonated beverages, too.

18

Forego the Fancy

Maybe while watching C-SPAN you've seen a copy of the president's budget. It's presented in four volumes every March, bound in blue, and runs, oh, 2,100 pages. A hard copy will set you back $200 and change.

How much attention do members of Congress pay to this document? About as much as potential donors will give to your fundraising materials.

You will reduce your own budget and be a lot more effective if you convey your message not on paper or a laptop or an iPad, but in person. For many major donors, campaign literature, as one wag put it, has as much impact as the sound of one hand clapping.

It's true that brochures, reports, and Q & A cards can play a role. For potential donors, they can create a favorable impression. For solicitors, they can be a stabilizing crutch. And for board members who take part in developing them, campaign materials can build camaraderie and focus attention on the organization's goals and objectives.

But always recognize print or electronic presentations for

what they are – supporting documents to your verbal presentation and nothing more. The basic ones to consider are:

- ❏ A case statement, typed, printed, or available as a PDF.
- ❏ A one-page outline of the case for the solicitor to use when talking with the prospect.
- ❏ A folder listing the various ways a prospect can give, covering the tax advantages and the mechanics of making outright and planned gifts of cash, securities, or property.
- ❏ A guide offering suggestions for soliciting prospects.
- ❏ A Q & A sheet, addressing the questions prospects are most likely to ask.
- ❏ A list of named gift opportunities.
- ❏ A pledge card or subscription form or letter of intent.

It's easy to get swept up in printed materials ("Don't you think we need our own logo?" "I prefer a darker shade of blue," "My neighbor's a freelance designer"). Making inconsequential decisions is always a fun distraction.

But it bears repeating: a brochure, whether hard copy or electronic, doesn't raise money. The solicitor does.

19

Wealth Alone Doesn't Determine

The *Guinness Book of World Records* memorialized her as the world's greatest miser.

Hetty Green, known as the Witch of Wall Street, made her millions through real estate, banking, and railroads. Her frugality was legendary. Hetty didn't use hot water, didn't heat her home, wore the same black dress every day, even refused to pay the doctor to treat her son's leg (which later had to be amputated).

Moral of the story: Regardless of income or assets, many find it hard to part ways with Ben, Grover or, god forbid, Woodrow (though the $100,000 bill is out of circulation now).

In terms of giving, we all think alike: Who's asking and for how much? Why me? For what purpose? Why now, and how soon again?

Things would be so easy otherwise. The *World Wealth Report* pegs the number of U.S. millionaires at just over three million. If giving depended solely on wealth, all you'd have to do is drop each one a line (or place a call for the personal touch).

Regrettably, it doesn't work that way. Regardless of their means, donors follow a logical progression. First they become interested in a cause, get more closely involved, and then deepen their commitment with a gift. That's the normal course of events.

You'd like it to be otherwise. But as Harold Seymour colorfully put it years ago: "You can't make a good pickle by squirting vinegar on a cucumber - it has to soak awhile."

20

That You Need, Won't Inspire

We've all encountered needy people. You know the type. They take everything personally, believe others can't possibly like them, feel they can't do anything right, and have never drunk from a half-full glass.

After a while they're exhausting to be around.

Remember that when approaching your potential donors. They don't like needy *organizations.* A study conducted by Bank of America in conjunction with The Center on Philanthropy at Indiana University showed that 87 percent of wealthy donors rank "sound business and operational practices" as important when determining which organizations to support.

In other words, dubious finances are a skull and crossbones warning. Noted consultant Kay Sprinkel Grace puts it this way: "Those who lament that money pours into great universities, major arts organizations, and other giant nonprofits rather than those that really 'need' it have to see the reason why: these organizations radiate success. They're professional, good at reporting their impact, and offer opportunities for people to fulfill their charitable instincts and have their investment protected."

In other words, donors give to solid organizations with worthy objectives. They want their gift to help save a life, enrich a child, feed a hungry person, shelter a teenage mother. That's why it's easier, for example, to raise money for a field trip than a furnace repair.

Sure you have needs – every organization does. But when asking for support, do so in a way that renders hope and makes people proud to be associated with your cause.

Again Ms. Grace: "A message of desperation may work once. Or even twice. But more than a few community orchestras and social service organizations have faded from the horizon when their frantic pleas for money ultimately fell on deaf ears. Those who had bailed them out let loose of the bucket."

21

Come a Little Closer

When you turn on the faucet for your morning shower, do you step right in? No. You wait for the water to heat up.

Well, that's a pretty good description of "cultivation." In fundraising, it means warming up your prospects before asking them to give.

Here's an example.

Not long ago, the National Museum of American History set out to raise money to preserve the *Jefferson Bible*, a handmade account of Jesus's teachings created by our third President.

With help from the staff, the museum board created a list of 18 people who they believed would be interested in the bible. Board members called each one and followed up with an invitation to a personal showing of Jefferson's book.

Thirteen eagerly appeared and were dazzled. One of the guests offered financial support even before he was asked. Another offered pro-bono help with future museum projects. The funds for the project were easily raised.

That's what cultivation does; it draws people closer to you, brings them into your circle.

It's unlikely you have an 18th century artifact, but you can build relationships in your own way. You might ask key prospects to tour your preserve, or attend a strategy session, or serve on a committee, or participate in an event. As a study by the University of Pennsylvania's Center for High Impact Philanthropy made clear, many if not most donors find their involvement in an organization "an absolute precondition" to making large gifts.

And almost anyone can be cultivated. If the New York-Presbyterian Hospital could woo Leona Helmsley, the legendary "Queen of Mean" who subsequently gave $25 million for medical research, then involving your perfectly pleasant prospects should be a breeze.

22

What You Don't Know Will Hurt You

This year, your odds of being struck by lightning are 1 in 700,000, according to National Geographic. It's a pretty safe bet you can slip on those galoshes and trudge off to work.

The odds of securing a BIG gift before you understand what makes your prospect tick? Well, no one's calculated them, but they're only slightly better, I imagine, than your being felled in a storm.

The point is, ignorance isn't bliss in fundraising. You have to learn a good deal about the people you plan to approach - their dreams, desires, and aspirations. Those in philanthropy understand that *prospect research* is usually the difference between success and failure.

Whether you're seeking a gift of $20,000 or $2 million, your first step is to identify your most promising prospects. These include your current and previous donors, of course, but pay attention as well to: users of your services; people who have shown an interest in your work; vendors; past and present board members; those with historical or family ties to your organization; employees; neighbors; and donors to similar causes.

The information you seek includes the following: Which of these individuals has the wherewithal to give; what are their giving habits; what relationship do they have with your organization; which aspect of your cause would most interest them; what cultivation is necessary; how much will you ask for; who has the respect of the prospect; and, who is the right person to do the asking?

Is all this time and effort worth it? Marc Keller of the University of Pennsylvania certainly thinks so. He recalls how background research helped uncover an engineering alumnus, the owner of a large energy technology company, who went on to pledge $20 million to found the school's nanotechnology center.

We can all hope lightning will strike in the form of an out of the blue, windfall gift. And it will ... eventually. The "infinite monkey theorem" states that a chimp typing keys at random for an infinite amount of time will almost certainly type a given text, such as Shakespeare's *Romeo and Juliet*.

All good things come to him who waits, you could say – assuming "him" has the time.

23

Who Leads, Influences Who Gives

Let's assume Larry Lucchino, President and CEO of the Boston Red Sox, isn't available – too drained from co-chairing the $1 billion campaign for the Dana-Farber Cancer Institute.

Ditto for Disney's President and CEO Bob Iger. His plate is full raising money for the Academy Museum of Motion Pictures.

Even former New York Jets quarterback, Chad Pennington, is already suited up. He's calling the plays at Marshall University's $30 million campaign to improve athletic facilities.

Who the heck is going to lead your campaign!?

I know! George Bailey.

You remember George from the classic Christmas movie, *It's a Wonderful Life.* Played by Jimmy Stewart, George is as solid as they come. He runs an important business in town, works long hours when needed, is generous to a fault, and commands respect from virtually everyone.

George would be a good campaign chair (if only he had

Mr. Potter's assets he'd be the *perfect* one).

Since celluloid chairs have drawbacks, what specific traits should you look for in a real-life campaign leader?

Andrea Kihlstedt, author of *How to Raise $1 Million (or More!) in 10 Bite-Sized Steps*, suggests these three: "A passion for the cause, personal generosity, and follow-through" And ALL three are necessary, she says.

"I've known organizations that have taken literally a year to fill the post – that's how daunting the job can be," says Kihlstedt.

But let's be optimistic and assume you identify a promising candidate sooner. Before handing over the gavel, you'll still want to ask yourself the following questions:

- ❏ Is this person experienced in organizing people, in working with committees?
- ❏ Is he or she a leader, someone who easily elicits loyalty?
- ❏ Will this person add credibility to your campaign and motivate others to participate?
- ❏ Will the person contribute financially and at what level?
- ❏ Will he or she solicit others?
- ❏ Does your candidate have the time and energy required? And, finally,
- ❏ Is the person an appropriate spokesperson for your cause?

According to Stephen Manzi, former campaign director

for the New York Public Library, the single most important factor behind successful major gifts campaigns "is a pervasive sense of optimism. Campaigns succeed when people believe they will succeed."

And no one is more important in setting that tone than your campaign chair.

If you're feeling rushed and considering charging ahead without a strong leader, once again Andrea Kihlstedt has some advice:

"A poor chair will drag you down. An okay chair will keep you afloat. But a great chair will give your campaign wings."

24

Time Commands

New York's Second Avenue Subway was originally proposed in 1929. Then something happened called the Great Depression.

Twenty-two years passed and, in 1951, voters got around to approving funds for the line's construction. But the money was diverted instead.

Fast-forward to 2005 and still another $1.3 billion was earmarked.

To this day work on the line continues.

Life has a way of stalling. Fundraising's no different.

Who among us - piece workers aside - doesn't procrastinate? The more time we have the longer we take.

As far as fundraising is concerned, the antidote is a campaign timetable; a reasonably firm schedule of who does what by when.

That means affixing start and finish dates to a host of campaign activities: Conducting a feasibility study, developing a case, recruiting leaders, researching prospects, developing a gift table, printing materials, approaching lead prospects, and much more.

If keeping your train moving weren't reason enough for a timetable, here's another: In major gifts fundraising, it's critical to follow a "big donor to small donor" sequence.

The reasoning is simple. You hope that Town Bank's $100,000 gift will raise the sights of Village Bank, which otherwise might give $50,000.

But as you would expect, big donors take longer to solicit. Spouses, attorneys, and brokers get involved. Your timetable needs to reflect this longer gestation period. Otherwise you'll hastily jump to smaller donors because your campaign seems stalled.

It would be nice if we all acted promptly. But until Big Pharma develops a Pronto Pill, go with a timetable. It's just the nudge most of us need.

25

Stay on Top
Or Go Under

According to a study by the University of California, Riverside, reported in *The Journal of the American Psychological Association*, conscientious people live longer. Two to four years longer, researchers say.

That's good news. It means you'll be doing your campaign leaders a favor by holding their feet to the fire. After all, you want them to live to a ripe old age.

Letting things slide is the probably the second most common reason campaigns fail (not enough people asking for sizable gifts is the first). The rush of adrenalin has faded, half or more of the goal is banked, summer vacations loom - whatever the reasons, campaigns lose their momentum.

That's understandable considering the length of some campaigns. Even Alex Rodriguez and Albert Pujols slump over the course of a long baseball season.

A batting cage won't help here, but there are strategies to prevent your campaign from grounding out:

❑ Have your chairs schedule regular report meetings with their leaders, and those leaders with their workers.

❑ Use a troubleshooting committee to focus on key problems such as unfinished solicitations of top prospects.

❑ At a specially-called meeting, have users of your services (children, patients, students, the elderly) speak of your organization's importance to their lives.

❑ Hold a rally, midway through the campaign, during which all chairs and leaders report their progress.

We all wish people would do the job they agreed to, without prodding. But that's expecting human nature to change. Put away the Taser, but an occasional jolt can move things along nicely.

26

Training Begets Bigger Gifts

Imagine being asked to swim a hundred meters ... *with your hands tied and your feet bound.*

Wannabe Navy SEALs have to do exactly that (as well as freefall at 35,000 feet, in the dark, with 200 pounds of gear strapped on).

Fortunately, your training as a solicitor is a notch less taxing.

Most likely it'll take a few hours and cover the three stages of a typical solicitation - preparing for the visit, the visit itself, and follow-up - and stress the need for you to:

- ❏ Make your own gift first (*see Chapter 28*)
- ❏ Know your case – the reason you're raising money.
- ❏ Visit your prospect in person.
- ❏ Listen, and focus on his or her interests.
- ❏ Be positive; there's no reason to apologize.
- ❏ Ask for a specific gift.

❏ Have a second or even third meeting if it's a
large gift you seek.

If you've raised money before and are confident you don't
need further training, here's a quick test. How would you
respond to a donor who says:

"Before you say a word, here's my gift."
"I'll happily give that; I thought you'd ask for more."
"I have little interest in your cause."

If you paused even slightly, attend the training.

27

The Secret to Success

If you've been to New Orleans's French Quarter, there's a good chance a hustler came up to you, pointed to your feet, and said, "Two dollars I know where you got those shoes." Figuring only the clerk at Sock 'n Soul knows for sure, you accept the bet. "On your feet!" says the con artist, holding his hand out to collect.

Here's a similar trick question. The last time you gave to a cause – *$20* says *I* know what motivated you.

Because somebody asked you!

Donors give for an assortment of reasons. According to a study by the Colorado Nonprofit Association, the top three are: they believe the organization is trustworthy (98 percent), they believe the organization is well-managed and effective (96 percent), and they feel the organization supports a cause they believe in (96 percent).

But even so, what sparks a gift in the first place is the fact that there you are, in the flesh, asking for it. The problem is that many of us are willing to do anything *but* ask.

Maybe we don't fully believe in the cause. Or we're afraid

we'll be turned down. Or we question our persuasive powers. Or we worry *we'll* be asked for a gift in return. Or the cumulus clouds are foreboding today.

The truth is, there will always be a knot in your stomach, which, funny enough, is all the more reason to feel proud. "Courage is being scared to death ... and saddling up anyway," said John Wayne.

You won't ever quell the fear, not fully at least, but you can control it if you are:

❏ Well-prepared
❏ Genuinely enthusiastic about the cause
❏ Have some leverage with the prospect
❏ Communicate a sense of urgency, and,
❏ Have made a generous gift yourself.

Here's something else to remember; some donors *like* to be asked. Jeff Brooks, author of *The Fundraiser's Guide to Irresistible Communications*, is one. A few years back, his mother succumbed to Parkinson's. And now Brooks is a regular donor to organizations fighting the disease - and happy to be asked.

"There's a way I can strike back at Parkinson's," he says, "I can defy it, take back some of what it stole, by giving to a nonprofit organization. It can't bring my mother back or erase the pain, but giving reorients me. I'm less a victim, more in control."

Keep Jeff in mind as you're about to knock on your donor's door.

28

Those Who Ask, Must First Give

Imagine an investment-savvy friend drops by, all excited about an upcoming IPO. "This is the surest thing since Google," he says. "You gotta buy it."

Tantalized by the prospect of easy money, you log onto Stocks r Us and ask how many shares your pal has bought. "None yet," he says, "but if I were you I'd load up!" With that ringing endorsement, you log off.

It's the same with fundraising. Before you can hope to persuade a friend or colleague to support your cause, you have to believe in it yourself. And nothing says conviction better than a generous gift.

Personal giving accomplishes two things (three if you count your organization's ledger): It makes you a more enthusiastic advocate, and gives you added leverage during your visit.

It's quite effective when you can say, "John, I've contributed $5,000 to this project myself. I believe it's that important. I'm asking you to join me." Think of the credibility gap if you're asked about your own level of support and you personally haven't given.

"Well, um, you see...."

That would be when your prospect logs off.

29

Not All Donors Are Equal

The median salary for a Pittsburgh ophthalmologist is just shy of $250,000.

For a college professor in Texas, the figure is $111,000

A head custodian in the California school system has to squeak by on $40,000.

Ours is the land of the free, not the financially equal.

We'll let economists untangle that. What's relevant here is that donors come in all sizes. And early in your campaign it's important to identify which hold the most promise for you.

Rating your potential donors, as this process is called, is especially important in light of the fact – borne out over 80 years of campaigning – that the lion's share of your support will come, as mentioned in Chapter 8, from the top 10 percent of your donors. These are the dealmakers or deal breakers.

The group doing the rating – ideally people of equal standing to the prospects – searches primarily for three pieces of information: the right amount to suggest to the prospect, his or her areas of interest, and who the best solicitor will be. Among the factors you'll consider are:

- ❏ How wealthy is the prospect?
- ❏ Does the person give to other charitable causes?
- ❏ How much and for how long?
- ❏ On this prospect's priority list how high would your organization be? And, lastly,
- ❏ Do any of your committee members have influence on the prospect?

Raters shouldn't be concerned with what prospects *might* give, or even whether they *will* give. What you want to learn from this session is what a person, if sufficiently motivated, *could* give in light of their personal circumstances.

In other words, you're trying to gauge the person's financial capacity and philanthropic intent – even disregarding negative feelings toward your organization, which you would hope to change through cultivation activities.

You can bet some board members will balk at prospect rating. They'll think it smacks of gossip. But that won't be the case if before you say or write anything, you ask yourself one simple question: 'Is this something I'd be embarrassed to have the prospect see or hear?'"

If it is, then simply heed the sage advice of Euripides: "Silence is true wisdom's best reply."

30

Each According to His Means

This book would be a lot more interesting if I used my whole brain. But like you, I'm stuck using 10 percent.

And I'd have an easier time typing this sentence if I stopped cracking my knuckles. It's making me arthritic.

Which, to tell you the truth, is turning my hair gray, the stress from it all.

I suspect you recognize these statements for what they are – commonly held misconceptions. (Actually we use all of our brains, just at different times; knuckle cracking is harmless; and aging turns our gray hair, not stress.)

Fundraising has misconceptions, too. Here's one: "If we ask each person for the same amount, our job will be a cinch." All it takes to raise $100,000, for example, is ask 100 people to give $1,000. Presto.

Wrongo.

Here's why. First, this one-size-fits-all "strategy" ignores reality. Not all of those 100 people will give. In fact, you'll need to approach three or four prospects to secure one gift.

Second, not everyone will contribute $1,000, which means to achieve an *average* gift of $1,000, you'll need gifts of far greater amounts.

Third, asking for $1,000 in effect limits those who could or would give $5,000 or even more.

If these aren't reasons enough, here's another: This approach is grossly unfair. Located at 420 Rodeo Drive, Beverly Hills, is Bijan, reputedly the world's most expensive store. You need an *appointment* to shop for its $15,000 suits (matching socks: $100). Would it really be fair to ask Leonardo DiCaprio, a Bijan patron, for the same $1,000 as the key grip in his movie, *Shelter Island*?

Recognize the one-size-fits-all approach for the misguided notion it is. Instead, research your prospects, carefully rate them, and then seek a generous and proportionate gift.

Keep in mind what Irving Warner, a veteran fundraiser, said years ago:

"The man who suggests you need 1,000 contributions of $10 each for your $10,000 project:

A) Knows arithmetic.

B) Thinks he's given you a brilliant solution.

C) Won't give more than $10."

31

Big Before Little

If you're a runner as I am, it matters whether that dog on your tail is a toothy German Shepherd or a mildly curious Pomeranian. You pay more attention to the big breeds. It's the same with fundraising, only you're doing the tailing this time.

The first people you want to approach are those with the most bite. Their gifts usually set the bar and influence those that follow.

I bet you've been influenced by lead gifts yourself, without noticing.

Say a school kid knocks on your door selling Christmas wrap. You like Connor, so, yes, you'll buy a roll or two. He hands you his clipboard and asks you to write your name and the amount of your purchase. Hmm, you notice your next door neighbor just ordered $25 worth. Ten bucks is what you have in mind. "Good luck," you say to freckle-faced Connor as he walks away, "hope my $25 helps." Such is the power of lead gifts.

Pursuing big gifts before little ones is the first principle of what's called *sequential* fundraising.

For the second principle, think back to those chocolate bars you yourself were "asked" to sell in school.

I bet you unloaded them the way I did: first to parents, then grandparents, a kindly aunt, a cousin or two, and maybe a sympathetic older sister. The few remaining bars were pedaled to neighbors.

That approach was natural. We sold to the people who were closest to us. They were the most likely to respond.

Turns out that effective fundraising follows the same pattern. Only in this case, it's the *organization's* family you sell to first, most notably the board, then staff, current donors, followed by other appropriate people, including dedicated volunteers and large-scale vendors.

This two-fold strategy, called "top down, inside out," is essential for two reasons: first, a relatively small number of donors will account for most of the money you raise and that's where your focus should be; and, second, those closest to you – your organization's family - are your best prospects.

But sequential fundraising *will* test your restraint.

A big gift almost always takes longer to secure than a smaller one. As a result, some board members and volunteers will grow impatient and want to skip to the next, lower level. If you do, you squander the powerful leverage sequential fundraising provides.

32

Teams Work

Imagine basketball star LeBron James going up against the Los Angeles Lakers – *by himself.*

There's no question "King James" would score some points. But boy would it be easier with a few teammates.

It's the same when matching up with your own Kobe Bryants. Go in pairs or threesomes. You'll fortify each other's resolve. And two heads are better than one for fielding any tricky questions.

Generally speaking, the following teams (listed in order of effectiveness) work best: volunteer and organization's CEO; volunteer and staff member; CEO and staff member. But if you feel more people are needed, bring them along. "Heck, bring a marching band if you need to," says Jerold Panas, who was once part of a team that asked for a *hundred million* dollar gift.

Not only will the team approach increase your effectiveness, it'll also serve your organization in other ways.

First, newer volunteers will become more familiar and comfortable with the asking process.

Second, more than one person will come to know important prospects - helpful if the solicitor you've relied upon is unavailable in the future.

Finally, your volunteers will simply have more fun when they share in the asking. And, as no less an authority than Dr. Seuss said, "Fun is good."

33

Overloaded Solicitors Underproduce

AND NOW FOR SOME BREAKING NEWS: The average weight of a woman's handbag has plummeted, reports Debenhams, the largest department store chain in Great Britain.

Just a few years ago, ladies were lugging eight pounds in their Miu Miu's. Now, thanks to lighter, multi-functional gadgets like the iPhone, the weight has dropped 57 percent - to a petite three-and-a-half pounds.

Everyone is happy – except for physical therapists.

Your solicitors will be pleased, too – and a lot more effective - if you don't overload them with prospects.

Considering the time spent making the appointment, visiting the prospect, and following up with a letter or phone call, even a small number of solicitations is time-consuming.

So what's the magic number? Experience shows that *five* is reasonable. Any more and your campaigners may resort to phone calls rather than visits.

Expect some enthusiastic workers to request more ("I'm good at this – give me 15 people"). The Italians have some advice worth recalling here: "Big mouthfuls often choke."

There will be plenty more prospects for these eager solicitors once they've completed their initial set of calls.

34

Make a Match

CNN calls her the "Rolls Royce of matchmaking."

And compared to a Silver Phantom - $380,000 MSRP – she is a bargain. Still, for Orly the Matchmaker's world-renowned services you'll have to pony up $100,000 (for matches with "royalty, famous stars or international celebrities," double that).

eHarmony this isn't.

Strangely enough Orly's tactics – making custom-made matches based on compatible interests, values, and goals - are exactly the ones you should use when matching your solicitors with your prospects.

As to the profile of the best solicitor, opinions vary. Some insist it's a peer of the prospect; others say the CEO's organizational grasp makes him the most effective; still others argue for program staff.

Regrettably, there's no right answer here. *But there is one constant.*

"To me it doesn't matter whether the person asking for the gift is a staff person, a volunteer, or a friend. It just needs to be someone I respect." That's what philanthropist Robert Saligman said, and his insistence on respect – call it integrity - is echoed by other big givers. Malin Burnham, a San Diego philanthropist and chairman of nine nonprofits, says "Nothing is more important than integrity."

For Orly, a successful match means $100,000 (else your money is refunded, she promises). For you and your organization, the right solicitor asking the right prospect could mean 10 times that amount – maybe more.

So, yes, the time and effort are most definitely worth it.

35

More Alike Than Not

Is there anything you can't find on the Internet!?

Visit similarminds.com/match and by answering a few simple questions you can discover if you and your hairdresser or chiropractor or Pilates instructor think alike. Good riddance to pesky conversations.

Alas, it's doubtful your prospects will take the quiz, but there is a sneaky-simple way to judge what they're thinking when you visit. You ask yourself this question: How would *I* feel if I were in their shoes?

You'll come to the conclusion that John and Justine, Eduardo and Elsa, Armand and Aida – even with their beach houses and trust funds - still share many of the same concerns and anxieties as you.

They're interested in helping, like you. They're busy and prefer candor, like you. They respond favorably to dedicated volunteers, like you. And they will give to worthwhile causes, the same as you.

You'd never know any of this by the way so many campaigns fence off their prospects, as if inviting them into the organization's family – giving them what some call the "institutional hug" – will somehow expose what you really are and dissuade them from giving.

Does that make sense?

When your potential donor visits the shoe store, she won't spend a nickel before trying on that pair of pumps. But she's going to give you a check for $5,000 or $50,000 or $500,000 before sizing up whether your organization is a good fit with her own desires and values? I don't think so.

You'd do exactly the same, which is the point.

The next time you call upon a would-be donor, here's a can't-miss strategy. See him as yourself. You wouldn't want to be glad-handed, strong-armed, or, worse, threatened with Lucifer's sword when asked for a gift. No surprise; he doesn't either.

You'd simply want the solicitor to speak from his heart.

36

No Apology Needed

"**A**sking means never having to say you're sorry."

Okay, that's not exactly what Ali MacGraw said to Ryan O'Neal in *Love Story* (for those who missed this 70s classic, it was "*Love* means never having to say you're sorry").

But the sentiment is the same.

You're a solicitor, not a supplicant. As fundraising counselor Kay Sprinkel Grace makes clear: "It's not begging when a donor's gift provides housing for the homeless, food for the hungry, scholarships for deserving students, or medical help for those suffering from chronic conditions. It's not begging when the organization, on whose behalf you are asking, is stable, accountable, and successful in its work. By no means is it begging; it is an investment you seek."

You have every reason to feel extremely proud. Not only does it take courage to do what you're doing, but asking on behalf of your cause is a selfless act.

In 2007, as New York construction worker Wes Autrey and his two young daughters waited for the subway, a 19-year-old film student went into convulsions, stumbled from the platform, and landed smack dab between the rails. Springing into action, Autrey leapt down and, with the train thundering in, flung himself over the student, pinning him down as the downtown local roared over their heads. A clearance of two inches spared their lives.

Mind you, your actions aren't harrowing like the "Subway Samaritan's," but there is a selfless quality to what you do as well. Whether you're raising money for a hospital or school or museum or rec center, in effect you're enriching - if not actually helping to heal or save - the lives of others, most of whom you don't know, and will never know.

There's no need to apologize for that.

37

Work Your Core

It's appealing that the Ford Taurus you're eyeing has tinted glass, a rearview camera, and a trunk big enough for a Viking stove. But for you, the car's central purpose - getting you to and from work safely and on time – is what really matters.

Similarly, what's under your organization's hood – namely, the variety of programs and projects you offer – isn't nearly as important to your prospect as your *engine*, namely, your core mission.

As Henry Rosso, founder of The Fund Raising School, put it, "your overarching mission is the magnet that attracts and holds the interest of major donors. It is more important than any single project or program, more important in fact than the history of your organization, the solicitor, your distinct offerings, or your project's aims."

Philanthropy master Jerold Panas confirms this in his book, *Mega Gifts*. Panas interviewed a host of million dollar donors and to a person they echoed the words of Marianne McDonald, for whom the McDonald Center at Sharp Healthcare is named: "There is nothing that could move me to making a large gift if

I don't believe in the mission of the organization and its significance."

Couldn't be more airtight, could it? (Incidentally, in his studies Panas discovered two factors tied for *second* place in prompting a gift: one is the organization's financial stability, the other is a high regard for staff, usually the CEO.)

Sell your mission first, with all the passion you can muster. Only then will you be ready to speak of specific programs or projects.

38

Get Personal

"She's just a little tike now - your soccer star. But it won't be long before I see you jumping up and down as she scores the winning goal on this very field we're raising money for. That's why I'm hoping we can count on your support."

How can you make your project personal for your prospective donor? That's a question you need to always ask prior to paying a visit.

Say you're raising money for Alzheimer's research. For lab scientists, Alzheimer's is all about genetic markers, neural connections, and blood diagnostics. But for your prospects it's something totally different. It's hope that they and their family will be spared this debilitating disease.

Or, perhaps your local library needs to raise money for WIFI and added shelving. Those things are important, but they're impersonal. What you're really selling is the opportunity your library offers to young minds, a place that teems with ideas and stokes curiosity.

And that blighted historic house you want to save? Visitors to the manse will boost the profits of nearby shops, the value of surrounding properties will rise, and the town will have a wonderful facility for weddings. Ears will perk up at that.

You can make this same "human case" for colleges, museums, hospitals, for virtually any organization. But to do so you have to know your "product" and your prospect. What are your specific aims, how do they relate to the community at large, and what about your work will particularly interest this person?

Connect those dots and you'll secure the gift.

39

Go Figure

Say you're approached by a fellow worker and asked to pitch in for the comptroller's wedding gift. The first question you typically ask is, "How much you have in mind?" or "What are others giving?"

What you're seeking is a frame of reference.

The same dynamic plays out when you approach prospects. They want a sense of what you're looking for or what their peers are giving.

Are you talking $500, $5,000, or $50,000, they want to know.

You need to be specific. To many, that can be unnerving. Heck, it's hard enough to ask for "any amount you can give" or "whatever you can afford," but the temerity of naming a number – that's like asking "How much you make a year, bud?"

But if you've done your homework – which is to say, you haven't plucked a figure from thin air – then you won't upset your prospect, especially if you phrase the request tactfully: "We're hoping you'll consider a gift in the range of $50,000" or "Will you consider joining me in giving $25,000 to this worthy cause?"

Another way to frame your request is to mention what others are giving, naming names if you've been given permission. Or, you can stress how your campaign needs several friends to contribute at a certain level and you're hoping the prospect will be among them. Here, you might actually share the gift table you developed (see Chapter 10).

When you bring your car in for service, the mechanic diagnoses the problem and gives you a quote. What if instead he said nothing? You wouldn't know whether you could afford the repair, or even if your car is worth fixing. It would make you uncomfortable - you'd also question the mechanic's ability.

Don't put your prospect in a similar position. Suggest the amount you have in mind, a "quote" if you will. No one's going to slam the hood on your fingers.

40

Ask or All Is Lost

Much of life seems to happen in stages - curiously enough, four stages.

In Buddhism, there are the four stages of enlightenment.

Biology students will recall the four stages of mitosis.

Apparently, there are even four stages of burnout (ahem, let's skip over that one).

It turns out that effective solicitations also involve four stages:

1) The introduction, including a bit of small talk.

2) Followed by a discussion that encourages your prospect to express her views of your organization.

3) Then your explanation of the need and the benefits that will accrue.

4) And finally the closing, when you ask for a gift.

Sailing through the first three stages is easy - the winds are brisk. But then you feel the boat lurch as the time to ask presents itself.

"On the timeline of fundraising, it's the smallest step," says one noted consultant. "But on the register of importance, all the other steps can be meaningless without it."

It'll never be easy. I didn't learn to swim until my 40s and I remember the day my instructor motioned me to the deep end and said "Jump." That's the angst you'll feel.

Certainly don't worry about any magic words. Say what feels comfortable for you. I myself like to phrase the request this way:

❏ Would you join with me in making a gift of...
❏ Would you become a part of this effort by making a gift of...
❏ We hope you will consider a gift of...

That way it's clear I'm hoping for support, not demanding it.

The trouble is, it might take your prospect 30 seconds or even a full minute to respond. He's thinking: "Can I afford this? Is this organization that important to me? Will they use my money wisely? Do I need to speak to my attorney first?"

It may be excruciating for you - this period of silence - but *don't interrupt his thoughts.* Pretend you're in Japan if you must, where a long pause during a negotiation is a traditional sign of respect.

Let your prospect sort through his real feelings. If you're going to advance this solicitation, those feelings are exactly what you need to hear now.

41

I Shall Return, Maybe

As you wait in the checkout line for the customer ahead of you to find his Depends coupon, you surely notice the candy bars, gum, miniature cookbooks, pen flashlights, even fingernail clippers all vying for your attention. Retailers know that impulse buys are good for business.

Some fundraising works that way, as when cashiers ask if you'll contribute a dollar to their cause of the month, or when Girl Scouts, stationed at the exits, make thick pleas for their Thin Mints.

But you're seeking *thoughtful* gifts, so the words you'll frequently hear after asking for $5,000 or $50,000 are … "I need to think about it."

Recall what we said earlier about the gestation period of big gifts and the need to consult spouses, attorneys, and brokers.

"I understand you need time to think it over," you reply with understanding.

But wait. Don't take your leave yet. Channel Detective Columbo.

You remember how Peter Falk's character - a dumb as a fox inspector for those who missed the Sunday night show - would casually turn on his way out and ask one last question. Only in your case you're probing for the answers to three questions:

1) Does the prospect feel your cause is worthy?
2) Does she feel you asked for an appropriate amount?
3) Is the timing somewhat problematic?

How your prospect responds – and remember this is a conversation, not an interrogation – will often reveal the reason or reasons for her hesitation. Perhaps she doubts the value of your cause, or feels you're asking for too much, or has tuition bills due in August, making the timing problematic.

If you're fortunate, you'll be able to resolve the matter quickly: "Would it help to postpone your gift until October?" But even when you can't fashion a quick solution – say, a spouse who needs to be consulted is away on business - the clues you pick up from asking these questions will be invaluable to your follow-up visit.

42

Gratitude to One and All

The story goes that when Booker T. Washington was raising money for Tuskegee Institute (now Tuskegee University) he received a letter from John D. Rockefeller offering a single dollar.

Insulting, you say? Not to Washington. He wrote Rockefeller a gracious thank-you and at the end of the year sent the oil man an accounting of what he'd done with every single penny.

It won't surprise you that Rockefeller began his real support of Tuskegee soon afterward.

There are plenty of reasons to express your gratitude, but four stand out.

First, it shows you're considerate. "Gratitude is the most exquisite form of courtesy," said French philosopher Jacques Maritain.

Second, it reflects well on your organization.

Third, satisfied donors (like John D.) are your best source

of future gifts.

Fourth, gratitude in the form of accountability is especially powerful.

In its *Heart of the Donor* study, the Russ Reid group confirmed the truth of this last reason. They found that 71 percent of donors continue giving because the organization "gave me information about exactly what my gift accomplished." Accountability yields loyalty.

It's something good salespeople understand.

My wife and I recently had new windows put in. As long as they keep the bugs out, who cares, a window's a window. Not to our installer. Six months after the job he called. "Windows okay? You happy with them?" Tight as a tick, we assured him, impressed with his follow-up.

What this successful contractor was saying was: "I appreciate your business, I'm accountable, and I'd like you as a future customer."

Think if you did the same with your donors - called occasionally, or sent a personal note. "Want to let you know that because of your gift our students were able to visit the anatomy exhibit yesterday. In fact, you'll be getting a thank-you note from some of them in a day or two."

Think that small gesture could create a lifetime donor?

You would be right.

43

Your Donor Is Waiting

No doubt you've heard Thomas Edison's description of genius.

A serial inventor who in addition to the light bulb produced the world's first recording (it was *Mary Had a Little Lamb* – no kidding), Edison said genius is 1 percent inspiration and 99 percent perspiration.

Fundraising has a ratio, too, only a little less constricted: it's 10 percent asking and 90 percent preparation. Since you've now reached page 101, this shouldn't surprise you.

By the time you're ready to ask, you will have involved the prospect in your work, shared your vision and goals, and documented the importance of your mission to the community and beyond.

And then?

Listen to what Kay Sprinkel Grace has to say:

"Something happens when you see a donor connect with the values, mission, and vision of your organization. It's as if there's an audible 'click.' Suddenly, the desires of your organization and those of the prospective donor are wedded."

So wedded, in fact, that Vartan Gregorian, who raised immense sums of money for Brown University and the New York Public Library, offered this surprising insight. "I would let donors know about my dreams and vision for the future," he said. "I explained how important the program was and the lives it affected. When I finished, it seemed I never had to ask. They always came forward with what they wanted to do. It had become their dream and vision."

An overstatement, perhaps, but a sentiment worth remembering. When you approach fundraising in a deliberate way, by the time you're ready to ask, your donors are ready to give.

44

An Evaluation Enlightens

For a college history exam, a friend of my daughter's was once asked to "Evaluate the cultural role of the papacy from its origins to the present day, concentrating on the social, political, economic, religious, and philosophical impact on Europe, America, Asia, and Africa. *Be brief and concise, yet specific*" [italics mine].

Thankfully, evaluating your campaign isn't remotely as challenging.

Of course, the best measure of your success is obvious: did you reach your goal? But considering your next campaign may be only (gulp) 12 to 24 months away, it's smart to dig a little deeper, especially since new faces will build upon your work.

To clarify where you succeeded or failed, here are the questions to ask:

Expenses
Where was money put to good use, where was it wasted?
Materials
Which campaign materials were useful, which were

seldom used?

Meetings

Were there too many, too few, and which kind were the most productive?

Solicitations

Which worked best, team solicitations or solo visits, volunteers or staff?

Future leaders

Which workers distinguished themselves and should be tapped for other posts in your organization?

If, in fact, your campaign failed, or didn't achieve what you hoped, you will want to look at the following as well:

Timing

Was your campaign poorly timed? For example, was a more popular organization soliciting your prospects ahead of you?

Commitment

Did your leadership grasp the importance of the campaign and accept its urgency?

Potential donors

Did you have enough legitimate prospects, those with some link to your organization, with the ability to give, and with interest in your cause?

Inner-family giving

Did your board of directors give generously and proportionately?

Realistic goal

Was your goal realistic, that is, was it based upon the pledges of your inner-family and the careful rating of your prospects? Was it in line with what your consultant suggested?

Publicity

Did you rely on publicity, rather than personal visits, to raise money?

Leadership

Did you have strong leadership that made a plan, stuck to deadlines, and followed up on loose ends?

If you visit the website, wordassociation.com, and type in "evaluation," the words that come up are "grades," "test," "assessment," "performance." Don't much care for the sound of them myself.

On the other hand, if you type in "pizza," you find "yum," "yummy," "food," "slice," and "pepperoni."

Hmm.

Call an evaluation meeting, make mine "the works," and I'll answer any question you have. Chances are your board members will, too.

Those who lead the next campaign will be notably grateful for your report.

ONE LAST THOUGHT

Simplicity Prevails

Talk about utter simplicity! The twist tie.

You find it in grocery stores - that little thin wire encased in plastic that secures your bag of green beans.

You don't think of somebody actually inventing it, but the U.S. Patent Office credits Gary Lowe and Terry Langland with the original idea in 1914.

Fundraising isn't as simple as a twist tie, but neither is it complicated. Through the years, many techniques have been tested. The ones that endure today allow you to raise the *most money* in the *shortest time* at the *least expense*.

I've discussed many in this book, from the need to recruit able leadership to prospect research to gift tables to the importance of suggesting a specific amount.

But even if you forget the fine points, you'll still succeed if you remember a few simple tips:

❑ Learn as much about your organization as you can
❑ Make your own generous gift first.
❑ Know your prospect.

❏ Visit him in person.
❏ Let him know how much you've given and
  ask for the amount you hope he'll give.
❏ Remain quiet and wait for a response.

Oh, and one other thing – recognize how very special you are.

Somewhere in the United States, there's a hall of fame for practically everyone and everything. There's a Burlesque Hall of Fame, a Cowboy Hall of Fame, a Cricket Hall of Fame, a Midget Auto Racing Hall of Fame, there's even an Insurance Hall of Fame (which I have to doubt charges admission).

But even though we're home to world renowned institutions - health, educational, cultural, civic, you name it - and even though they rely on people like you for their very existence - as of this writing there is no hall of fame for fundraising volunteers.

Shameful isn't it?

When Bill Gates or George Soros or Warren Buffet or Christy Walton finally get around to building it, one thing is certain.

A prominent place in the Hall will be reserved most especially for you.

Certainly you deserve it.

ABOUT THE AUTHOR

David Lansdowne has spent his professional life in the non-profit sector, serving in a wide variety of development and administrative positions for educational, cultural, and health organizations throughout the United States.

THE GOLD STANDARD IN BOARD BOOKS

Asking Jerold Panas, 112 pp., $24.95, ISBN 9781889102351

It ranks right up there with public speaking. Nearly all of us fear it. And yet it's critical to our success. *Asking for money.* This landmark book convincingly shows that nearly everyone, regardless of their persuasive ability, can become an effective fundraiser if they follow Jerold Panas' step-by-step guidelines.

The Ultimate Board Member's Book
Kay Sprinkel Grace, 120 pp., $24.95, ISBN 9781889102399

A book for *all* nonprofit boards: those wanting to operate with maximum effectiveness, those needing to clarify exactly what their job is, and, those wanting to ensure that all members are 'on the same page.' It's all here in jargon-free language: how boards work, what the job entails, the time commitment, the role of staff, effective recruiting, de-enlisting board members, and more.

How to Raise $1 Million (or More) in 10 Bite-Sized Steps
Andrea Kihlstedt 104 pp., $24.95, ISBN 9781889102412

Raising a million dollars is easier than you think, says Andrea Kihlstedt. It's a matter of simplifying the process. Do that and you expel the anxiety. Kihlstedt prescribes 10 bite-sized steps. And with nearly three decades of experience and scores of campaigns to draw from, she has plenty of street cred.

The Board Member's Easier Than You Think Guide to Nonprofit Finances
Andy Robinson & Nancy Wasserman, 111 pp., $24.95, ISBN 9781889102436

With the possible exception of "How do I avoid fundraising?" a board member's most commonly unasked question is, "What do all these numbers mean, and what am I supposed to do with them?" Financial planning and budgeting combine all of our money taboos with that common math disorder, math phobia. But authors Andy Robinson and Nancy Wasserman help trustees and their staff colleagues confront and address this fear - with wisdom, clarity, humor, and humility.

www.emersonandchurch.com

THE GOLD STANDARD IN BOARD BOOKS

The 11 Questions Every Donor Asks
Harvey McKinnon, 112 pp., $24.95, ISBN 9781889102375

A watershed book, *The 11 Questions* prepares you for the tough questions you'll inevitably face from prospective donors. Harvey McKinnon identifies 11 such questions, ranging from "Why me?" to "Will my gift make a difference?" to "Will I have a say over how you use my gift?"

The Fundraising Habits of Supremely Successful Boards
Jerold Panas, 108 pp., $24.95, ISBN 9781889102474

In his storied career, Jerold Panas has worked with more than 3,000 boards, all the while helping them to surpass their campaign goals of $100,000 to $100 million. Funnel every ounce of that experience and wisdom into a single book and what you end up with is *The Fundraising Habits of Supremely Successful Boards*, the brilliant culmination of what Panas has learned firsthand about boards that excel at the task of resource development.

How to Make Your Board Dramatically More Effective,
Starting Today Gayle Gifford, 114 pp., $24.95, ISBN 9781889102450

This could be the most productive hour your board ever spends. Sixty minutes is all it takes to read *How to Make Your Board Dramatically More Effective, Starting Today.*Gayle Gifford poses a host of key questions. By answering them, your board can tell instantly what it's doing right, what's it's doing wrong, and where it can stand improvement.Suited to any board that isn't perfect.

Fundraising Mistakes that Bedevil All Boards (and Staff Too)
Kay Sprinkel Grace 110 pp., $24.95, ISBN 9781889102405

Over the past 70 years, organizations of all kinds have tested literally hundreds of fundraising techniques and strategies. Some have succeeded beyond expectations, but too many approaches have failed The result? Untold hours are wasted, causes go unfunded, and disappointment and frustration demoralize volunteers and staff everywere. Grace seeks to end these costly blunders once and for all.

www.emersonandchurch.com

Copies of this and other books from the publisher
are available at discount when purchased in
quantity for boards of directors or staff. Call 508-
359-0019 or visit www.emersonandchurch.com

Emerson
& Church
PUBLISHERS

15 Brook Street • Medfield, MA 02052
Tel. 508-359-0019 • Fax 508-359-2703
www.emersonandchurch.com